Create your own Masterpiece
on a journey through art

Text by Kathryn Cave

Illustrations by Melvin Bramich

F

FRANCES LINCOLN
CHILDREN'S BOOKS
in association with the
National Gallery of Art, Washington

Create your own Masterpiece © Frances Lincoln Limited 1994
Text and illustrations © Frances Lincoln Limited 1994
Drawings by Melvin Bramich

All paintings reproduced by courtesy of the Board of Trustees,
National Gallery of Art, Washington. (See also picture index.)

The publishers would like to thank the following for granting a licence
to reproduce in black and white the pictures on page 48:

Beasts of the Sea © Succession H. Matisse/DACS 1994;

The Bicycle Race © ADAGP, Paris and DACS, London 1994;

The Farm © ADAGP, Paris and DACS, London 1994;

Number 1, 1950 (Lavender Mist) © 1993 Pollock-Krasner Foundation/ARS, New York.

First published in Great Britain in 1994 and in the USA in 2005 by
Frances Lincoln Children's Books, 4 Torriano Mews,
Torriano Avenue, London NW5 2RZ

www.franceslincoln.com

Distributed in the USA by Publishers Group West

British Library Cataloguing in Publication Data available on request

ISBN 978-1-84507-450-0

Printed in China
3 5 7 9 8 6 4 2

Would you like to create your own masterpiece? As you take a journey through this book, every page gives you the opportunity to make your own work of art.

Before you start, you'll need to pack essentials for the voyage - paints, pencils, crayons, felt-tips, scissors, glue - and of course, this book. Then zoom off at the wheel of your car to meet adventure, excitement and perhaps even danger on a fast-moving journey through art. You can set sail to a mysterious island, go riding on a ranch, or camp out in the desert - you'll find something new to do, and draw, around every corner.

Every time you turn the page, the story takes a new twist. The notes and picture outlines give you suggestions about what to draw, but it's up to you to fill in the details of your adventures, using paints, pens, cut-outs or anything else you can think of to make your book look as colourful and exciting as possible.

Each of the stops on the way is based on an image from a painting in the National Gallery of Art, in Washington, D.C., USA. You can see the paintings if you visit the gallery, but there is also a small picture of each one inside the back cover.

So, pack your paint box, and get ready to go. Turn the pages - and have a good trip!

Remember me!

You're leaving home to see the world! Before you go, you ask your favourite artist to paint your portrait. You give the picture to your family to remember you by.

- Fill the frame with the portrait your artist paints.
- Write your name in the space at the bottom of the frame - or make up a new name for yourself and write that there instead.

If you want some ideas, you could look at the paintings by Rembrandt Peale, Amedeo Modigliani and Mary Cassatt reproduced inside the back cover.

Pack a picnic

It's your last night at home, and you plan to set out first thing in the morning. Before you go to bed, you go down to the kitchen and pack a delicious picnic lunch to take with you on the journey. You put in lots of fruit and - what else?

• Draw in the rest of the kitchen table and all the things you are going to pack to eat and drink on your picnic.

• Underneath the table there is something you *really* don't want to forget - you never travel without it. Show what it is in your picture.

The fruit comes from a painting by Paul Cézanne called *Still Life with Apples and Peaches*. You can see the whole painting inside the back cover.

Goodbye!

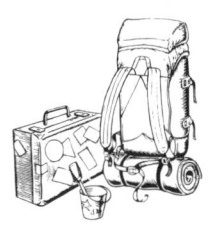

You're off at last! Who knows what lies ahead - excitement, adventure, danger? You can't wait to find out. All the same, halfway down the road you turn and look back through the gateway.

- Draw the view you see of the home you are leaving behind.
- Someone is waving goodbye from a window. Put them in your picture too.

The road and gateway come from a painting by Vincent van Gogh called *Farmhouse in Provence, Arles*. You'll find it inside the back cover. There is also a painting by Edward Hopper which might give you some ideas.

By the roadside

You pick up your car and drive all morning. Suddenly you see the ideal place to stop for lunch. You pull in off the road and enjoy your picnic. Then you go for a walk and see wonderful plants and butterflies.

- Fill the empty pages of your book with drawings and paintings of the fantastic plants you can see in the picnic area.
- The butterflies have the most brilliant colours you have ever seen, and each one is different. Show them resting or fluttering around the plants in your picture.

The plants and butterfly are from *A Bouquet of Flowers with Insects* by Pierre Joseph Redouté. You'll find it in colour inside the back cover.

Cartoon time

The person who last stayed in your hotel room left a newspaper behind. When you see the cartoon on the front page, you burst out laughing.

- Draw in the rest of the cartoon as you imagine it.
- Give the characters speech bubbles so that we can all share the joke. Write the words first. Then draw bubbles around the words.

The characters are from a cartoon by the French artist Honoré Daumier. You can read the translation of his original caption below the cartoon inside the back cover.

Breakdown

Your car made odd noises all morning,
and now it has broken down outside
a strange farm, miles from anywhere.
Luckily the farmer has a telephone,
so you can call the repair truck.
While you wait for the truck to
arrive . . .

• Draw what you can see of the farm:
house, barn, animals - everything.
• Colour your drawing in with the
brightest felt-tip pens you can find.

This is part of Joan Miró's painting *The Farm*.
The whole painting is reproduced inside
the back cover.

Dawn in the desert

You take a wrong turning late at night and never reach your hotel. You find a dry cave and settle down in your sleeping bag for the night. Next morning, you wake up at sunrise to discover you are not alone!

• Draw or paint whatever or whoever you find sharing your cave.
• Show the spectacular view of the desert you can see framed in the rocky cave mouth.

The cave is from Giovanni Bellini's *Saint Jerome Reading*. If you find the painting inside the back cover, you'll be able to compare your view of the landscape with his.

Riding into trouble

You need a break from driving, so you stop at a ranch to go riding instead. It's lucky for you that you're a skilled rider, because you run into something unexpected.

- Draw or paint yourself on the horse.
- Something or someone has given your horse a dreadful fright - show what it is in your picture.

Saint George was the original rider of this horse, in Raphael's painting *Saint George and the Dragon*. You'll find the painting reproduced inside the back cover.

Undiscovered country

The road you've been following ends at the water's edge. You leave your car and journey on by boat. Just over the horizon is an island that isn't on any map.

- Draw or paint what the island looks like from near the shore.
- While you are gazing at the island, you are surprised to see a strange boat sailing in your direction. Where does it come from and who can be in it? Add the boat to your picture.

Your boat is from Fitz Hugh Lane's *Lumber Schooners at Evening on Penobscot Bay*. You can find the painting inside the back cover.

Gold coins

The inhabitants of the island have
strange and wonderful designs on
their coins. You're so impressed by
them that you copy four of the designs
into your book.

- Fill in the blank coins opposite with
designs and mottoes of your own.
- Your brand new coins are for a
brand new country - invent a name
for it and write it underneath
your coin designs.

The coin designs on this page are from etchings
by Jaques Callot. There are more inside the
back cover.

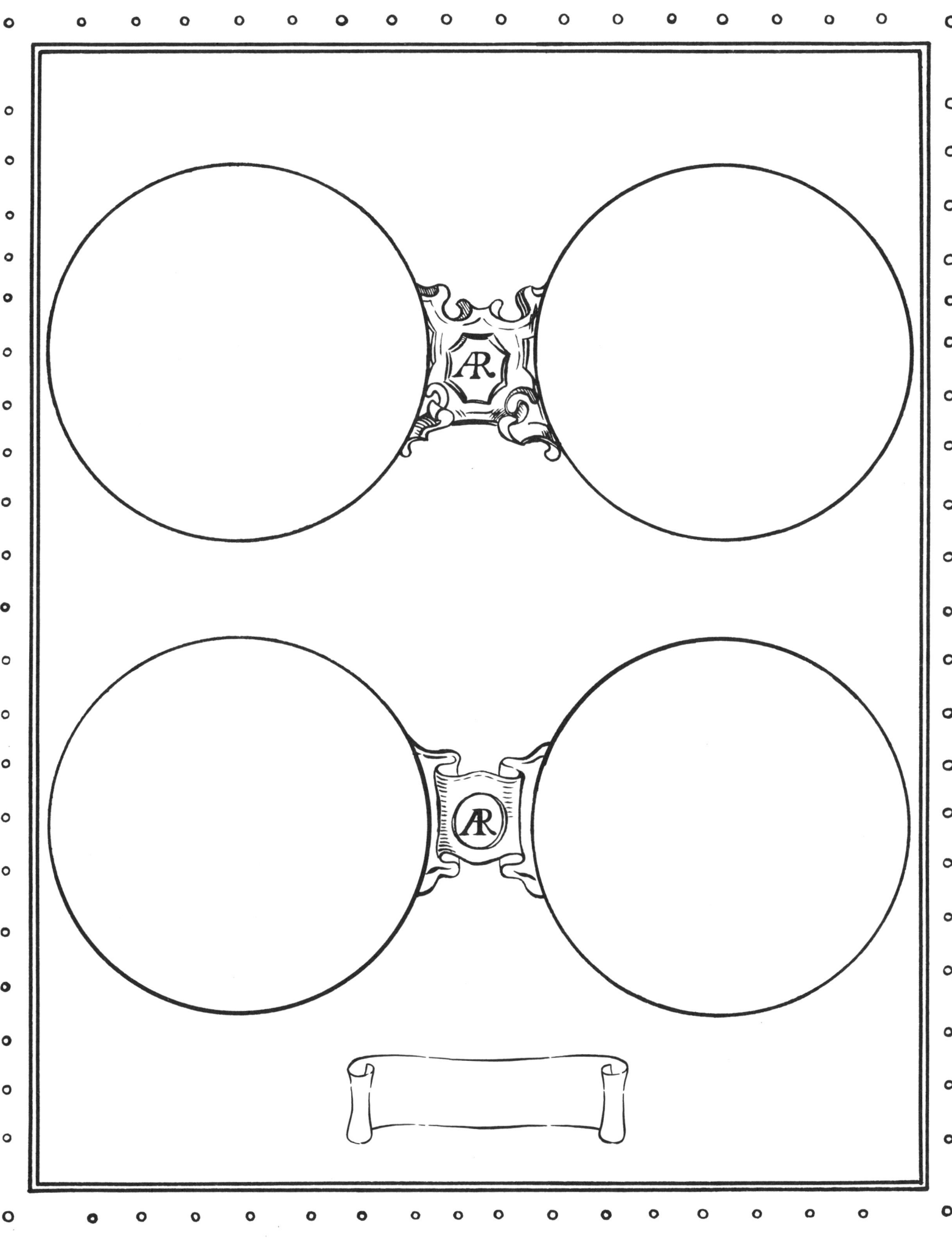

Sea beasts

A storm blows up when you're in the boat again, and it's too rough to draw or paint. Luckily you have scissors and a stick of glue with you, and there's a box of old magazines and postcards in your cabin, so you have everything you need to make a collage of all the creatures of the sea.

• Make lots of cut-out sea creatures: jellyfish, octopuses, eels, sharks, whales, and fish of every shape and colour - and glue them onto the opposite page.

• Cut out wavy strips of paper to make seaweed for your underwater world and glue them onto your collage.

The designs opposite come from a collage by Henri Matisse, *Beasts of the Sea*. You can see the whole collage inside the back cover.

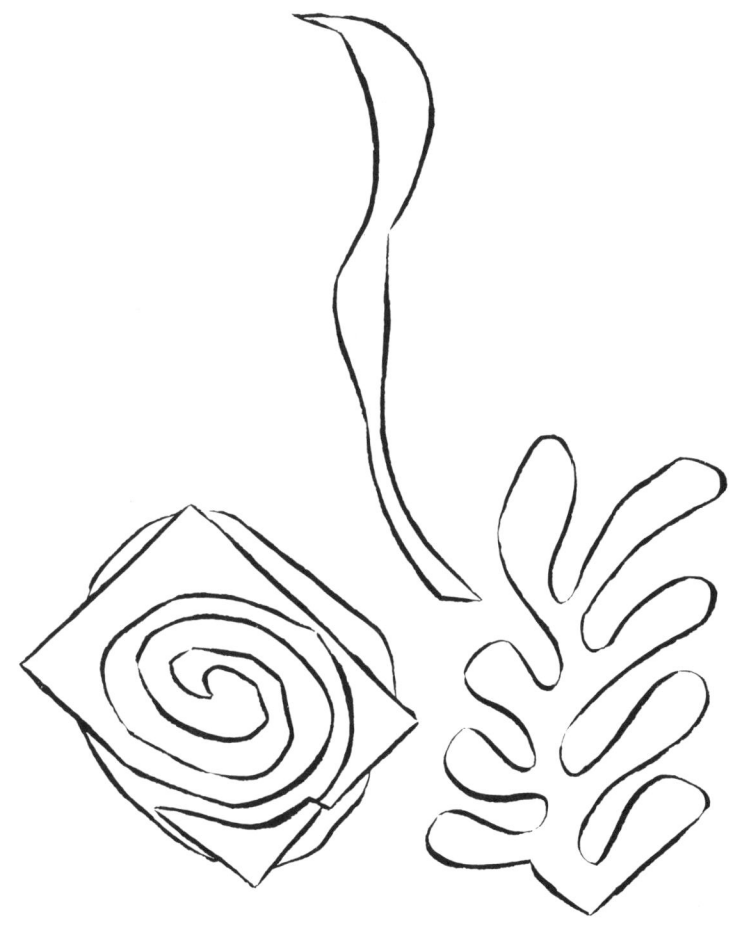

A sailor's story

The boat sails on, and on, and on...
The days seem endless, and you've
read all your books twice already.
You spend the afternoons listening
to stories the crew tell of adventures
they've had at sea. One of the stories
is so vivid you can almost see it
happening.

● Part of the story is shown on the
opposite page. Fill in the rest of
the details to show what is going on.

The people in this boat come from a painting
by John Singleton Copley called *Watson and the
Shark*. If you want to see the rest of the story,
look for the painting inside the back cover.

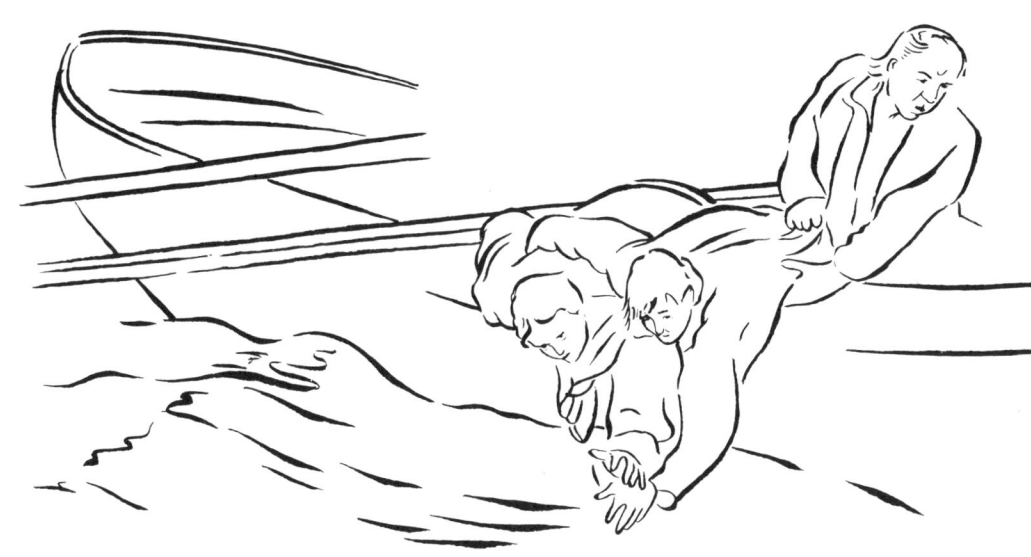

Landfall!

You can see land at last. You can't wait to get your feet on to dry ground again. As soon as you've fixed up a place to stay, you go off for a stroll around town.

- Paint in the buildings you can see around the harbour, using a small paintbrush and applying colour in dots like the rest of the picture.
- It's a wonderful day: the sky is blue and the water shimmers in the bright sunlight. Use bigger blobs of colour to paint in the sea and the sky in your picture.

The lighthouse is from Georges Seurat's *The Lighthouse at Honfleur*. It is reproduced inside the back cover.

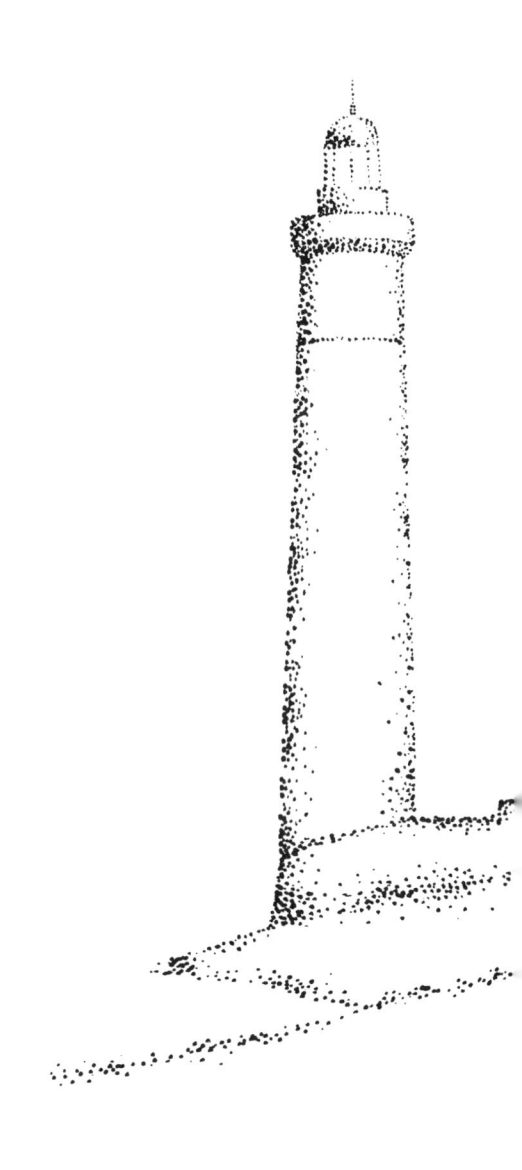

Evening

You're back on the road again - but
it feels like the road to nowhere.
At sunset, you finally come to a house
and stop to ask for directions.

- What does the lonely house look
like? Draw in the rest of the house -
walls, windows, roof, shutters and all.
- What is the man looking at? Draw it
in your picture.

The house and the person are from Edward
Hopper's *Cape Cod Evening*. To see what else
the artist put in the painting, look inside
the back cover.

Across the bridge

You're back on the right track, and you've found a great place to stay, overlooking a river. You can see several boats from your window, and a bridge, and a town on the other side of the water.

- Draw or paint the bridge and the buildings on the far shore.
- Make some more sailing boats from scraps of paper and glue them onto your picture.

The boat is from Claude Monet's *The Bridge at Argenteuil*. It is reproduced inside the back cover.

Strange birds

Walking deep in the forest, you see some birds you recognize - and some you don't!

- Fill these torn-out pages from your notebook with sketches of the strange and colourful birds you see.
- Invent a name for each bird, and write it underneath the picture.

The bird on this page and *Cardinal Grosbeak* opposite were painted by John James Audubon. You'll find them both inside the back cover.

CARDINAL GROSBEAK

Wheels

You're out exploring the streets of a new town one quiet evening when you hear the sound of wheels. You barely have time to jump out of the way before a group of cyclists sweeps past with a crowd of people and vehicles following.

• Draw or paint the other road-users you see streaming past.

The bicyclists come from Lyonel Feininger's *The Bicycle Race*, reproduced inside the back cover.

Winter's kingdom

It's winter here, although your family and friends back home are still enjoying the sun.

• Add some more wintry-looking trees and buildings to this picture of the view from your hotel room.

• Before you've finished the picture, it starts to snow again. Tear some white paper into small pieces and stick them over your picture to look like snowflakes.

This scene comes from *Skating Scene* by John Toole. You'll find it inside the back cover.

An afternoon snack

After a day of fun in the snow, you feel really hungry. Hurrying back to your hotel, you pass a pastry shop. Its window display is the most tempting you have ever seen…

• Fill the spaces with pictures of the delicious-looking cakes and biscuits you see in the window.

• You can see the shopkeeper through the window too. Show him standing behind the cakes.

The cakes are from Wayne Thiebaud's *Cakes*, reproduced inside the back cover.

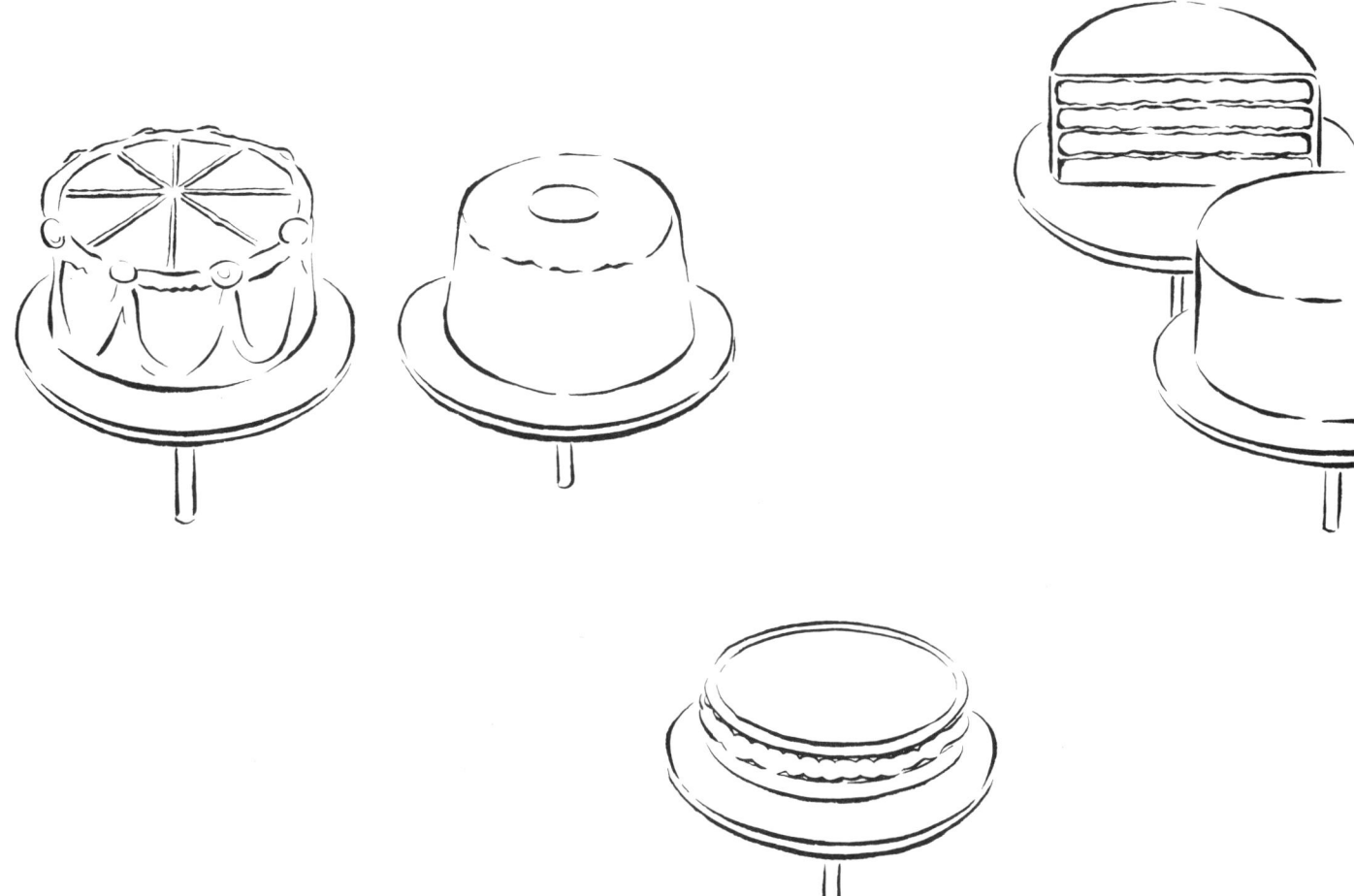

Amazing art

The last city you visit has a marvellous art gallery with lots of exciting modern paintings.

- Fill the space on the opposite page with squiggles, swirls, straight lines, blobs, splashes, cut-outs - whatever you like! - to create a wild and wonderful abstract painting all your own.
- When you've finished, make an unusual frame for your painting.

If you need a little inspiration, you might like to look at the paintings by Jackson Pollock and Juan Gris, inside the back cover.

City skyline

It's time to head for home at last.
As your train pulls out of the station,
you get a wonderful view of the bright
city skyline through the window.

- Fill in the rest of the skyline.
There could be spires, turrets, domes,
whatever you like!
- What else can you can see from
the train? Shops? Houses? Churches?
Statues? Factories? Show them all in
your picture.

The skyline and buildings on the page opposite
come from a painting by Auguste Renoir, called
Pont Neuf, Paris. You can find it inside the flap
on the back cover.

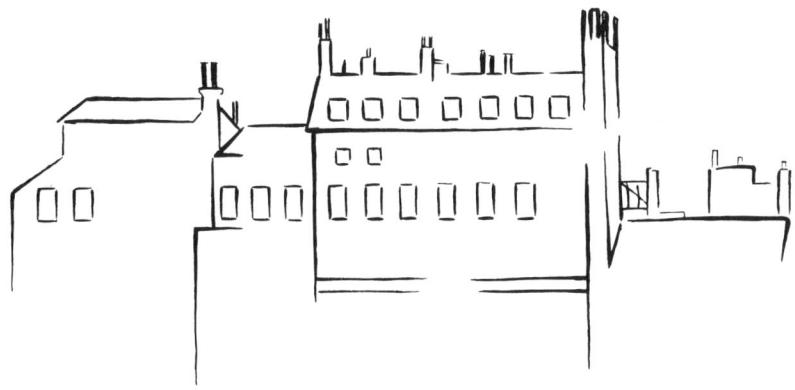

Welcome home

Your train pulls into your home station,
and you can't wait to see your family
and friends again. As you walk towards
the grand station exit, you catch sight
of them waiting outside.

• Draw or paint the people you love -
waving, calling, cheering - happy to
welcome you home!

This imposing archway was never actually built!
Jan van der Heyden painted it as part of
An Architectural Fantasy, reproduced inside
the back cover.

Jaques Callot (1592 - 1635)

The Coins 1662

ROSENWALD COLLECTION

Henri Matisse (1869 - 1954)

Beasts of the Sea 1950

AILSA MELLON BRUCE FUND

© Succession H Matisse/DACS 1994

Lyonel Feininger (1871 - 1956)

The Bicycle Race 1912

COLLECTION OF MR AND MRS PAUL MELLON

© ADAGP, Paris and DACS, London 1994

Honoré Daumier (1808 - 1879)

It is rather flattering to have so many pupils!... 1838

ROSENWALD COLLECTION

Joan Miró (1893 - 1983)

The Farm 1921 - 1922

GIFT OF MARY HEMINGWAY

© ADAGP, Paris and DACS, London 1994

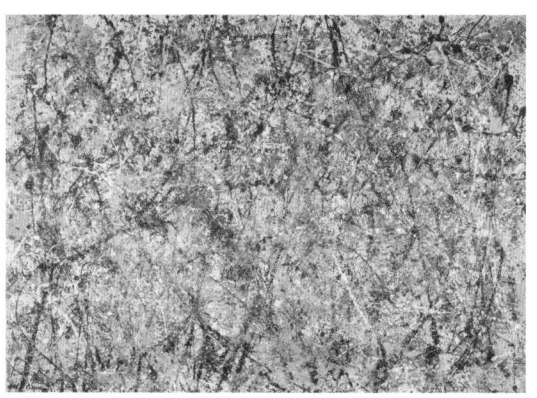

Jackson Pollock (1912 - 1956)

Number 1, 1950 (Lavender Mist) 1950

AILSA MELLON BRUCE COLLECTION

© 1993 Pollock-Krasner Foundation/ARS, New York